MW01168781

FLASHCARD BOOKS

HOUSEHOLD ITEMS

ENGLISH

to

FRENCH

FLASHCARD BOOK

BLACK & WHITE EDITION

HOW TO USE:

- READ THE ENGLISH WORD ON THE FIRST PAGE.

- IF YOU KNOW THE TRANSLATION SAY IT OUT LOUD.

- TURN THE PAGE AND SEE IF YOU GOT IT RIGHT.

- IF YOU GUESSED CORRECTLY, WELL DONE!
IF NOT, TRY READING THE WORD USING THE PHONETIC PRONUNCIATION GUIDE.

- NOW TRY THE NEXT PAGE.
THE MORE YOU PRACTICE THE BETTER YOU WILL GET!

BOOKS IN THIS SERIES:
ANIMALS
NUMBERS SHAPES AND COLORS
HOUSEHOLD ITEMS
CLOTHES

ALSO AVAILABLE IN OTHER LANGUAGES INCLUDING:

FRENCH, GERMAN, SPANISH, ITALIAN,

RUSSIAN, CHINESE, JAPANESE AND MORE.

WWW.FLASHCARDEBOOKS.COM

Cushion

Le coussin

Luh koo-sahn

Arm Chair

Le fauteuil

Luh foo-toy

Sofa

Le canapé

Luh can-a-pay

Chair

La chaise

Lah shez

Fireplace

La cheminée

Lah she-mi-nay

Magazine

La revue

Lah reuh-voo

PC

La PC / l'ordinateur

Lah pey-sey lore-dee-nah-terr

Television

La télévision

lah tey-ley-vi-ziohn

Remote Control

La télécommande

Lah tey-ley-kom-mohnd

Speakers

Les haut-parleurs

lay oh-par-lur

Laptop

L'ordinateur portable

loor-di-na-tor poor-tabl

Fish Tank

L'aquarium

laa-kwa-riom

Light blub

L'ampoule

lome-pool

Rug

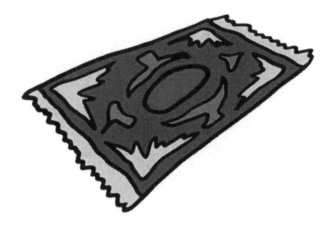

Le tapis

luh taa-pee

Clock

L'horloge

loor-lozh

Keys

Les clés

Lay k-ley

Iron

Le fer à repasser

Luh fer-a-re-pa-sey

Plant

La plante

lah plohnt

Table

La table

lah ta-bl

Photo Frame

Le cadre photo

luh ka-dr-fo-to

Light Switch

L'interrupteur

lahn-te-ru-ptor

Balloon

Le ballon

luh ba-ll-ohn

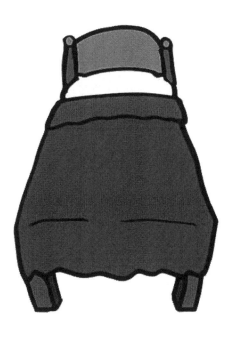

Bed

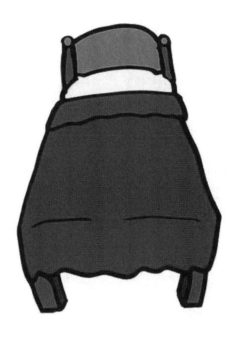

Le lit

luh lee

Double Bed

Le lit double

luh lee-doo-bl

Bunk Bed

Le lit superposé

luh lee-siu-per-po-zey

Lamp

La lampe

lah lohmp

Pillow

L'oreiller

loor-rey-iyeh

Duvet

La couette

lah coo-ett

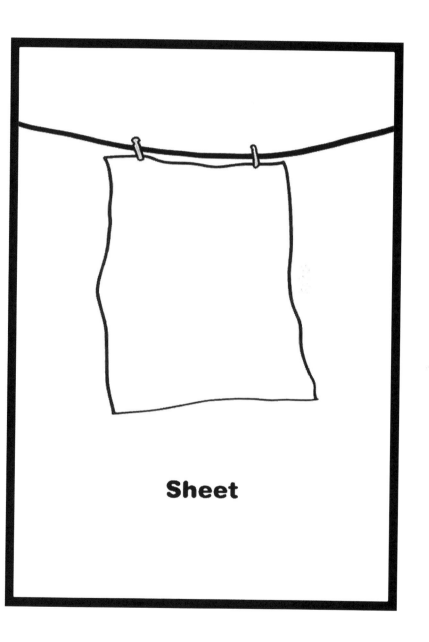

Sheet

Le drap

luh dra

Alarm Clock

Le réveil

luh rey-vei

Crib

Le lit d'enfant

luh lee dohn-fohn

Wardrobe

L'armoire

laar-mwar

Drawers

Les tiroirs

(lay tee rwar)

Cell Phone

Le telephone portable

(luh tey-ley-fon por-tabl)

Light

La lumière

lah liu-mier

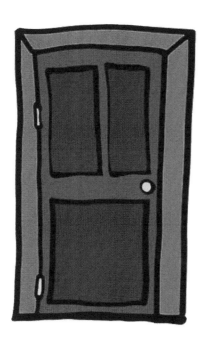

Door

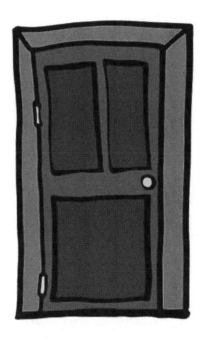

La porte

lah port

Window

La fenêtre

lah fe-netr

Roof

Le toit

luh twa

Door Bell

La sonnette

lah so-nett

Newspaper

Le journal

luh zhoor-nal

Oven

Le four

luh foor

Microwave

Le micro-ondes

luh mik-ro ohnd

Toaster

Le grille-pain

le gri-pahn

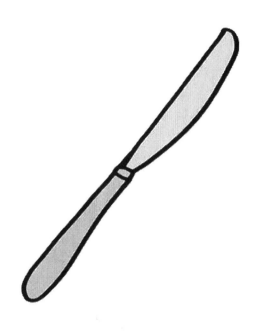

Butter Knife

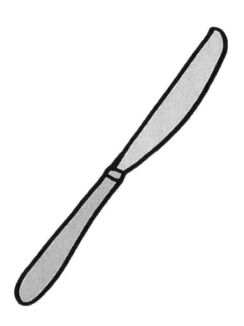

Le couteau à beurre

luh koo-toh ah bur

Fork

La fourchette

lah foor-sheyt

Spoon

La cuillère

lah kwee-yer

Kitchen Sink

L'évier de cuisine

ley-vi-yay de kwi-zeen

Cupboard

Le placard

luh pla-kar

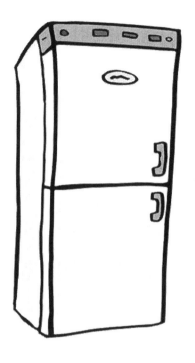

Fridge

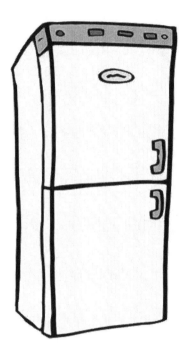

Le frigo

luh free-goh

Kettle

La bouilloire

lah booi-war

Pans

Les casseroles

lay kas-rohl

Frying Pan

La poêle à frire

lah pwal ah frir

Knife

Le couteau

luh koo-toh

Dishwasher

Le lave-vaisselle

luh lave-vaisselle

Washing up Liquid

Le liquide vaisselle

luh li-kid we-sell

Washing Machine

Le machine à laver

luh ma-shin a la-vey

Oil

L'huile

luh-oo-ill

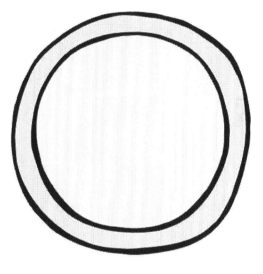

Plate

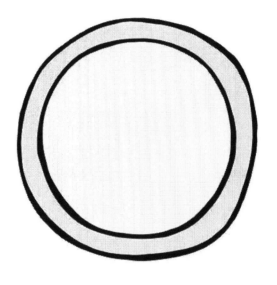

L'assiette

laah-ssiet

Cup

La tasse

lah tass

Broom

Le balai

luh ba-ley

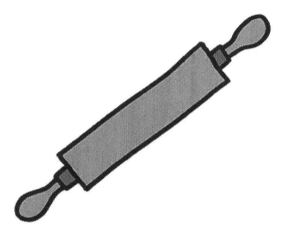

Rolling Pin

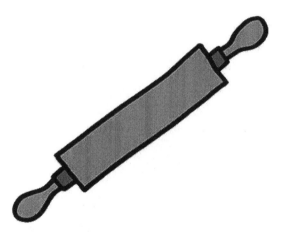

Le rouleau à pâtisserie

luh roo-loh a pa-tee-sree

Toothbrush

La brosse à dents

lah brohs a dohn

Toothpaste

Le dentifrice

luh dohn-tee-freez

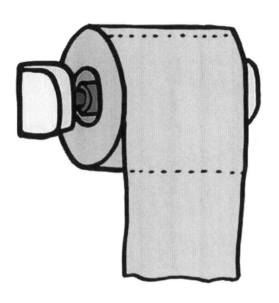

Toilet Paper

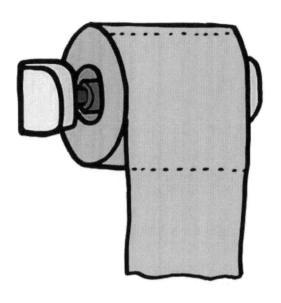

Le papier toilette

luh pah-pie twa-lett

Shower

La douche

la doosh

Soap

Le savon

luh sa-vohn

Tap

Le robinet

luh roh-bee-ney

Toilet

Les toilettes

lay twa-lett

Sink

Le lavabo

luh la-va-boh

Bath

Le bain

luh bahn

Shampoo

Le shampooing

luh sham-poo-ing

Sponge

L'éponge

ley-pohnzh

Hairdryer

Le sèche-cheveux

luh seysh-she-vu

Pencil Sharpener

Le taille-crayon

luh tai-krey-yohn

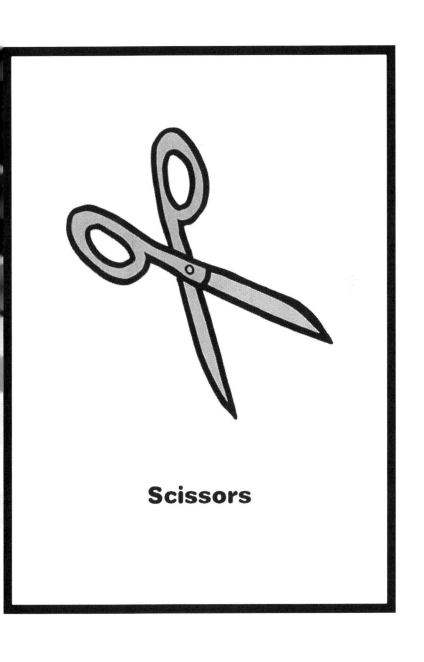

Scissors

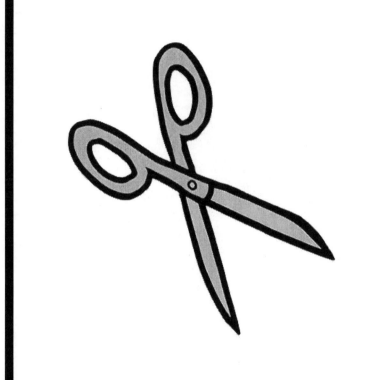

Les ciseaux

lay si-zo

Book Case

La bibliothèque

la bib-li-oh-tek

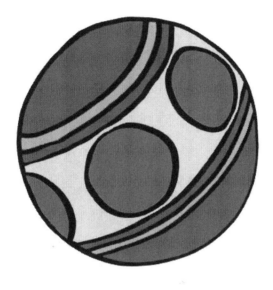

Ball

La balle

lah bal

Doll

La poupée

lah poo-pey

Teddy Bear

L'ours en peluche

loors ohn pe-lush

Castle

Le château

luh sha-toh

Sandwich

Le sandwich

luh sohn-dwich

Breakfast Cereal

Les céréales

lay se-re-all

Milk

Le lait

luh ley

Apple

La pomme

lah pomm

Hammer

Le marteau

luh mar-toh

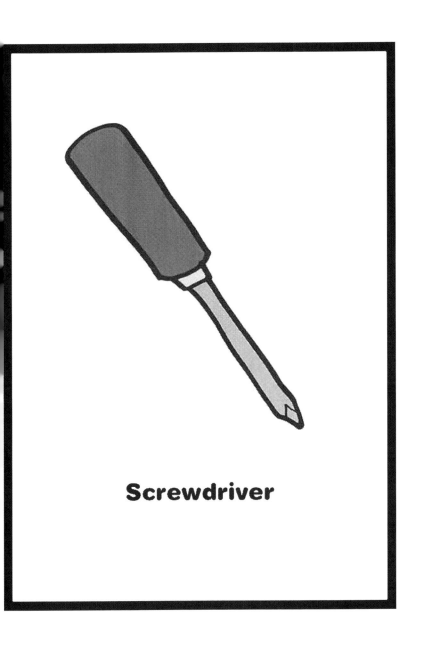

Screwdriver

Le tournevis

luh toor-ne-vees

Screw

La vis

lah vee

Nails

Les clous

lay kloo

Wrench/Spanner

La clé à molette

lah kley-ah-moh-lett

Shovel

La pelle

lah peyll

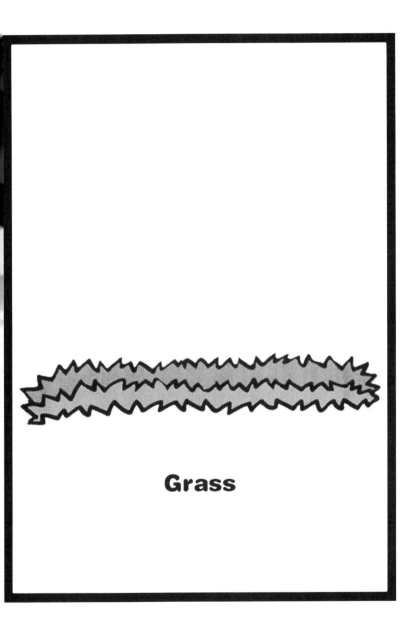

Grass

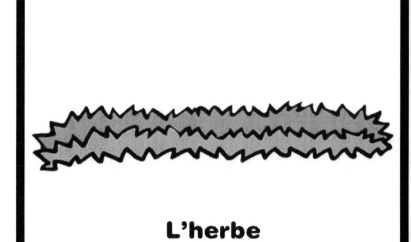

L'herbe

Ierb

Tree

L'arbre

larbr

Green House

La serre

lah sair

Lawn Mower

La tondeuse à gazon

lah tohn-doz a ga-zohn

Hose

Le tuyau

luh twi-yoh

Wheelbarrow

La brouette

lah broo-ett

Rake

Le râteau

luh rah-toh

ALL IMAGES COPYRIGHT ANTONY BRIGGS 2017

if you have enjoyed this book, please leave an Amazon review.

Thanks

63988406R00110

Made in the USA
Middletown, DE
08 February 2018